let's cook

wok & stir-fry

Siân
Davies

p

Contents

Chicken, Spring Green & Yellow Bean Stir-Fry

Yellow bean sauce is made from yellow soy beans and is available in most supermarkets.
Try to buy a chunky sauce rather than a smooth sauce for texture.

Serves 4

INGREDIENTS

2 tbsp sunflower oil
450 g/1 lb skinless, boneless chicken
   breasts
2 cloves garlic, crushed

1 green (bell) pepper
100 g/3^1/2 oz/1^1/2 cups mangetout
   (snow peas)
6 spring onions (scallions), sliced,
   plus extra to garnish

225 g/8 oz spring greens or cabbage,
   shredded
160 g/5^3/4 oz jar yellow bean sauce
50 g/1^3/4 oz/3 tbsp roasted cashew
   nuts

1 Heat the sunflower oil in a large preheated wok.

2 Using a sharp knife, slice the chicken into thin strips.

3 Add the chicken to the wok together with the garlic. Stir-fry for about 5 minutes or until the chicken is sealed on all sides and beginning to turn golden.

4 Using a sharp knife, deseed the green (bell) pepper and cut into thin strips.

5 Add the mangetout (snow peas), spring onions (scallions), green (bell) pepper strips and spring greens or cabbage to the wok. Stir-fry for a further 5 minutes or until the vegetables are just tender.

6 Stir in the yellow bean sauce and heat through for about 2 minutes or until the mixture starts to bubble.

7 Scatter with the roasted cashew nuts.

8 Transfer the chicken, spring green and yellow bean stir-fry to warm serving plates and garnish with extra spring onions (scallions), if desired. Serve the stir-fry immediately.

COOK'S TIP

Do not add salted cashew nuts to this dish otherwise, combined with the slightly salty sauce, the dish will be very salty indeed.

Chicken Stir-Fry with Cumin Seeds & Trio of (Bell) Peppers

Cumin seeds are more frequently associated with Indian cooking, but they are used in this Chinese recipe for their earthy flavour. You could use $^1/_2$ tsp of ground cumin instead.

Serves 4

INGREDIENTS

450 g/1 lb boneless, skinless chicken breasts
2 tbsp sunflower oil
1 clove garlic, crushed
1 tbsp cumin seeds
1 tbsp grated fresh ginger root

1 red chilli, deseeded and sliced
1 red (bell) pepper, deseeded and sliced
1 green (bell) pepper, deseeded and sliced
1 yellow (bell) pepper, deseeded and sliced

100 g/3$^1/_2$ oz/1 cup beansprouts
350 g/12 oz pak choi or other green leaves
2 tbsp sweet chilli sauce
3 tbsp light soy sauce
deep-fried crispy ginger, to garnish (see Cook's Tip)

1 Using a sharp knife, slice the chicken breasts into thin strips.

2 Heat the oil in a large preheated wok.

3 Add the chicken to the wok and stir-fry for 5 minutes.

4 Add the garlic, cumin seeds, ginger and chilli to the wok, stirring to mix.

5 Add all of the (bell) peppers to the wok and stir-fry for a further 5 minutes.

6 Toss in the beansprouts and pak choi together with the sweet chilli sauce and soy sauce and continue to cook until the pak choi leaves start to wilt.

7 Transfer to warm serving bowls and garnish with deep-fried ginger (see Cook's Tip).

COOK'S TIP

To make the deep-fried ginger garnish, peel and thinly slice a large piece of root ginger, using a sharp knife. Carefully lower the slices of ginger into a wok or small pan of hot oil and cook for about 30 seconds. Remove the deep-fried ginger with a slotted spoon, transfer to sheets of absorbent kitchen paper and leave to drain thoroughly.

Stir-Fried Chicken with Lemon & Sesame Seeds

Sesame seeds have a strong flavour which adds nuttiness to recipes.
They are perfect for coating these thin chicken strips.

Serves 4

INGREDIENTS

4 boneless, skinless chicken breasts
1 egg white
25 g/1 oz/2 tbsp sesame seeds
2 tbsp vegetable oil

1 onion, sliced
1 tbsp demerara sugar
finely grated zest and juice of
  1 lemon

3 tbsp lemon curd
200 g/7 oz can waterchestnuts
lemon zest, to garnish

1 Place the chicken breasts between 2 sheets of cling film (plastic wrap) and pound with a rolling pin to flatten. Slice the chicken into thin strips.

2 Whisk the egg white until light and foamy.

3 Dip the chicken strips into the egg white, then into the sesame seeds until coated evenly.

4 Heat the oil in a large preheated wok.

5 Add the onion to the wok and stir-fry for 2 minutes or until just softened.

6 Add the sesame-coated chicken to the wok and continue stir-frying for 5 minutes, or until the chicken turns golden.

7 Mix together the sugar, lemon zest, lemon juice and the lemon curd and add the mixture to the wok. Allow the lemon mixture to bubble slightly without stirring.

8 Drain the waterchestnuts and slice them thinly, using a sharp knife. Add the waterchestnuts to the wok and heat through for 2 minutes. Transfer to serving bowls, garnish with lemon zest and serve hot.

COOK'S TIP

Waterchestnuts are commonly added to Chinese recipes for their crunchy texture as they do not have a great deal of flavour.

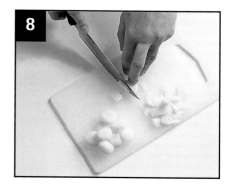

Chinese Chicken Rice

*This is a really colourful main meal or side dish
which tastes just as good as it looks.*

Serves 4

INGREDIENTS

350 g/12 oz/1³/₄ cups long-grain
  white rice
1 tsp turmeric
2 tbsp sunflower oil
350 g/12 oz skinless, boneless
  chicken breasts or thighs, sliced

1 red (bell) pepper, deseeded and
  sliced
1 green (bell) pepper, deseeded and
  sliced
1 green chilli, deseeded and finely
  chopped

1 medium carrot, coarsely grated
150 g/5¹/₂ oz/1¹/₂ cups beansprouts
6 spring onions (scallions), sliced,
  plus extra to garnish
2 tbsp soy sauce

1 Place the rice and turmeric in a large saucepan of lightly salted water and cook until the grains of rice are just tender, about 10 minutes. Drain the rice thoroughly and press out any excess water with double thickness paper towels.

2 Heat the sunflower oil in a large preheated wok.

3 Add the strips of chicken to the wok and stir-fry over a high heat until the chicken is just beginning to turn a golden colour.

4 Add the (bell) peppers and chilli to the wok and stir-fry for 2–3 minutes.

5 Add the rice to the wok, a little at a time, tossing well after each addition until well combined.

6 Add the carrot, beansprouts and spring onions (scallions) to the wok and stir-fry for a further 2 minutes.

7 Drizzle with the soy sauce and mix well.

8 Garnish with extra spring onions (scallions), if wished and serve at once.

VARIATION

Use pork marinated in hoisin sauce instead of the chicken, if you prefer.

Stir-Fried Chicken with Cashew Nuts & Yellow Bean Sauce

Chicken and cashew nuts are a great classic combination, and this recipe is no exception. Flavoured with yellow bean sauce it is a quick and delicious dish.

Serves 4

INGREDIENTS

450 g/1 lb boneless chicken breasts
2 tbsp vegetable oil
1 red onion, sliced

175 g/6 oz/1^{1}/$_{2}$ cups flat mushrooms, sliced
100 g/3^{1}/$_{2}$ oz/^{1}/$_{3}$ cup cashew nuts

75 g/2 ^{3}/$_{4}$ oz jar yellow bean sauce
fresh coriander (cilantro), to garnish
egg fried rice or plain boiled rice, to serve

1 Using a sharp knife, remove the excess skin from the chicken breasts if desired. Cut the chicken into small, bite-sized chunks.

2 Heat the vegetable oil in a preheated wok.

3 Add the chicken to the wok and stir-fry for 5 minutes.

4 Add the red onion and mushrooms to the wok and continue to stir-fry for a further 5 minutes.

5 Place the cashew nuts on a baking tray (cookie sheet) and toast under a preheated medium grill (broiler) until just browning – this brings out their flavour.

6 Toss the toasted cashew nuts into the wok together with the yellow bean sauce. Allow the sauce to bubble for 2–3 minutes.

7 Transfer to warm serving bowls and garnish with fresh coriander (cilantro). Serve hot with egg fried rice or plain boiled rice.

COOK'S TIP

Chicken thighs could be used instead of the chicken breasts for a more economical dish.

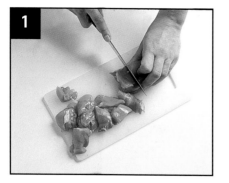

Stir-Fried Beef & Vegetables with Sherry & Soy Sauce

*Fillet of beef is perfect for stir-frying as it is so tender
and lends itself to quick cooking.*

Serves 4

INGREDIENTS

2 tbsp sunflower oil
350 g/12 oz fillet of beef, sliced
1 red onion, sliced
175 g/6 oz courgettes (zucchini),
 sliced diagonally
175 g/6 oz carrots, thinly sliced
1 red (bell) pepper, deseeded and
 sliced

1 small head Chinese leaves,
 shredded
150 g/5^1/$_2$ oz/1^1/$_2$ cups beansprouts
225 g/8 oz can bamboo shoots,
 drained
150 g/5^1/$_2$ oz/^{1}/$_2$ cup cashew nuts,
 toasted

SAUCE:
3 tbsp medium sherry
3 tbsp light soy sauce
1 tsp ground ginger
1 clove garlic, crushed
1 tsp cornflour (cornstarch)
1 tbsp tomato purée

1 Heat the sunflower oil in a large preheated wok.

2 Add the beef and onion to the wok and stir-fry for 4–5 minutes or until the onion begins to soften and the meat is just browning.

3 Using a sharp knife, trim the courgette (zucchini) and slice diagonally.

4 Add the carrots, (bell) pepper, and courgettes (zucchini) and stir-fry for 5 minutes.

5 Toss in the Chinese leaves, beansprouts and bamboo shoots and heat through for 2–3 minutes, or until the leaves are just beginning to wilt.

6 Scatter the cashews nuts over the stir-fry.

7 To make the sauce, mix together the sherry, soy sauce, ground ginger, garlic, cornflour (cornstarch) and tomato purée. Pour the sauce over the stir-fry and toss until well combined. Allow the sauce to bubble for 2–3 minutes or until the juices start to thicken.

8 Transfer to warm serving dishes and serve at once.

Beef with Green Peas & Black Bean Sauce

This recipe is the perfect example of quick stir-frying ingredients for a delicious, crisp, colourful dish.

Serves 4

INGREDIENTS

450 g/1 lb rump steak
2 tbsp sunflower oil
1 onion

2 cloves garlic, crushed
150 g/5^{1}/$_2$ oz/1 cup fresh or frozen peas

160 g/5 ^{3}/$_4$ oz jar black bean sauce
150 g/5 ^{1}/$_2$ oz Chinese leaves, shredded

1 Using a sharp knife, trim away any fat from the beef. Cut the beef into thin slices.

2 Heat the sunflower oil in a large preheated wok.

3 Add the beef to the wok and stir-fry for 2 minutes.

4 Using a sharp knife, peel and slice the onion.

5 Add the onion, garlic and peas to the wok and stir-fry for a further 5 minutes.

6 Add the black bean sauce and Chinese leaves to the mixture in the wok and heat through for a further 2 minutes or until the Chinese leaves have wilted.

7 Transfer to warm serving bowls and serve immediately.

COOK'S TIP

Chinese leaves are now widely available. They look like a pale, elongated head of lettuce with light green, tightly packed crinkly leaves.

COOK'S TIP

Buy a chunky black bean sauce if you can for the best texture and flavour.

Stir-Fried Garlic Beef with Sesame Seeds & Soy Sauce

Soy sauce and sesame seeds are classic ingredients in Chinese cookery.
Use a dark soy sauce for fuller flavour and richness.

Serves 4

INGREDIENTS

25 g/1 oz/2 tbsp sesame seeds
450 g/1 lb beef fillet
2 tbsp vegetable oil

1 green (bell) pepper, deseeded and
   thinly sliced
4 cloves garlic, crushed

2 tbsp dry sherry
4 tbsp soy sauce
6 spring onions (scallions), sliced
noodles, to serve

1 Heat a large wok until it is very hot.

2 Add the sesame seeds to the wok and dry fry, stirring, for 1–2 minutes or until they just begin to brown. Remove the sesame seeds from the wok and set aside until required.

3 Using a sharp knife, thinly slice the beef.

4 Heat the oil in the wok. Add the beef and stir-fry for 2–3 minutes or until sealed on all sides.

5 Add the sliced (bell) pepper and crushed garlic to the wok and continue stir-frying for 2 minutes.

6 Add the sherry and soy sauce to the wok together with the spring onions (scallions) and allow to bubble, stirring occasionally, for about 1 minute.

7 Transfer the garlic beef stir-fry to warm serving bowls and scatter with the dry-fried sesame seeds. Serve hot with boiled noodles.

COOK'S TIP

You can spread the sesame seeds out on a baking tray (cookie sheet) and toast them under a preheated grill (broiler) until browned all over, if you prefer.

Sweet Chilli Pork Fried Rice

*This is a variation of egg fried rice which may be served
as an accompaniment to a main meal dish.*

Serves 4

INGREDIENTS

450 g/1 lb pork tenderloin
2 tbsp sunflower oil
2 tbsp sweet chilli sauce, plus extra
  to serve
1 onion, sliced

175 g/6 oz carrots, cut into thin
  sticks
175 g/6 oz courgettes (zucchini), cut
  into sticks
100 g/3^1/$_2$ oz/1 cup canned bamboo
  shoots, drained

275 g/9^1/$_2$ oz/4^3/$_4$ cups cooked long-
  grain rice
1 egg, beaten
1 tbsp chopped fresh parsley

1 Using a sharp knife, slice the pork thinly.

2 Heat the sunflower oil in a large preheated wok.

3 Add the pork to the wok and stir-fry for 5 minutes.

4 Add the chilli sauce to the wok and allow to bubble, stirring, for 2–3 minutes or until syrupy.

5 Add the onions, carrots, courgettes (zucchini) and bamboo shoots to the wok and stir-fry for a further 3 minutes.

6 Add the cooked rice and stir-fry for 2–3 minutes, or until the rice is heated through.

7 Drizzle the beaten egg over the top of the fried rice and cook, tossing the ingredients in the wok, until the egg sets.

8 Scatter with chopped fresh parsley and serve immediately, with extra sweet chilli sauce, if desired.

COOK'S TIP

For a really quick dish, add frozen mixed vegetables to the rice instead of the freshly prepared vegetables.

Pork Fillet Stir-Fry with Crunchy Satay Sauce

Satay sauce is easy to make and is one of the best known and loved sauces in Oriental cooking. It is perfect with beef, chicken or pork as in this recipe.

Serves 4

INGREDIENTS

150 g/5^1/$_2$ oz carrots
2 tbsp sunflower oil
350 g/12 oz pork neck fillet, thinly
  sliced
1 onion, sliced
2 cloves garlic, crushed

1 yellow (bell) pepper, deseeded and
  sliced
150 g/5^1/$_2$ oz/2^1/$_3$ cups mangetout
  (snow peas)
75 g/3 oz/1^1/$_2$ cups fine asparagus
chopped salted peanuts, to serve

SATAY SAUCE:
6 tbsp crunchy peanut butter
6 tbsp coconut milk
1 tsp chilli flakes
1 clove garlic, crushed
1 tsp tomato purée

1 Using a sharp knife, slice the carrots into thin sticks.

2 Heat the oil in a large wok. Add the pork, onion and garlic and stir-fry for 5 minutes or until the lamb is cooked through.

3 Add the carrots, (bell) pepper, mangetout (snow peas) and asparagus to the wok and stir-fry for 5 minutes.

4 To make the satay sauce, place the peanut butter, coconut milk, chilli flakes, garlic and tomato purée in a small pan and heat gently, stirring, until well combined.

5 Transfer the stir-fry to warm serving plates. Spoon the satay sauce over the stir-fry and scatter with chopped peanuts. Serve immediately.

COOK'S TIP

Cook the sauce just before serving as it tends to thicken very quickly and will not be spoonable if you cook it too far in advance.

Sweet & Sour Pork

Everyone loves sweet and sour pork, a classic Chinese dish. Tender pork pieces are fried and served in a crunchy sauce. This dish is perfect served with plain rice.

Serves 4

INGREDIENTS

450 g/1 lb pork tenderloin
2 tbsp sunflower oil
225 g/8 oz courgettes (zucchini)
1 red onion, cut into thin wedges
2 cloves garlic, crushed
225 g/8 oz carrots, cut into thin sticks

1 red (bell) pepper, deseeded and sliced
100 g/3^1/$_2$ oz/1 cup baby corn corbs
100 g/3^1/$_2$ oz button mushrooms, halved
175 g/6 oz/1^1/$_4$ cups fresh pineapple, cubed

100 g/3^1/$_2$ oz/1 cup beansprouts
150 ml/^{1}/$_4$ pint/^{2}/$_3$ cup pineapple juice
1 tbsp cornflour (cornstarch)
2 tbsp soy sauce
3 tbsp tomato ketchup
1 tbsp white wine vinegar
1 tbsp clear honey

1 Using a sharp knife, thinly slice the pork tenderloin.

2 Heat the oil in a large preheated wok.

3 Add the pork to the wok and stir-fry for 10 minutes, or until the pork is completely cooked through and beginning to turn crispy at the edges.

4 Meanwhile, cut the courgettes (zucchini) into thin sticks.

5 Add the onion, garlic, carrots, courgettes (zucchini), (bell) pepper, corn cobs and mushrooms to the wok and stir-fry for a further 5 minutes.

6 Add the pineapple cubes and beansprouts to the wok and stir-fry for 2 minutes.

7 Mix together the pineapple juice, cornflour (cornstarch), soy sauce, ketchup, wine vinegar and honey.

8 Pour the sweet and sour mixture into the wok and cook over a high heat, tossing frequently, until the juices thicken. Transfer the sweet and sour pork to serving bowls and serve hot.

COOK'S TIP

If you prefer a crisper coating, toss the pork in a mixture of cornflour (cornstarch) and egg white and deep fry in the wok in step 3.

Stir-Fried Lamb with Black Bean Sauce & Mixed (Bell) Peppers

Red onions add great colour to recipes and are perfect in this dish, combining with the colours of the (bell) peppers.

Serves 4

INGREDIENTS

450 g/1 lb lamb neck fillet or boneless leg of lamb chops
1 egg white, lightly beaten
25 g/1 oz/4 tbsp cornflour (cornstarch)
1 tsp Chinese five spice powder

3 tbsp sunflower oil
1 red onion
1 red (bell) pepper, deseeded and sliced
1 green (bell) pepper, deseeded and sliced

1 yellow or orange (bell) pepper, deseeded and sliced
5 tbsp black bean sauce
boiled rice or noodles, to serve

1 Using a sharp knife, slice the lamb into very thin strips.

2 Mix the egg white, cornflour (cornstarch) and Chinese five spice powder together in a large bowl. Toss the lamb strips in the mixture until evenly coated.

3 Heat the oil in a large preheated wok. Add the lamb and stir-fry over a high heat for 5 minutes or until it begins to crispen around the edges.

4 Using a sharp knife, slice the red onion. Add the onion and (bell) pepper slices to the wok and stir-fry for 5–6 minutes, or until the vegetables just begin to soften.

5 Stir the black bean sauce into the mixture in the wok and heat through.

6 Transfer the lamb and sauce to warm serving plates and serve hot with freshly boiled rice or noodles.

COOK'S TIP

Take care when frying the lamb as the cornflour (cornstarch) mixture may cause it to stick to the wok. Move the lamb around the wok constantly during stir-frying.

Garlic-infused Lamb with Soy Sauce

*The long marinating time allows the garlic to really penetrate the meat,
creating a much more flavourful dish.*

Serves 4

INGREDIENTS

450 g/1 lb lamb loin fillet
2 cloves garlic
2 tbsp groundnut oil

3 tbsp dry sherry or rice wine
3 tbsp dark soy
1 tsp cornflour (cornstarch)

2 tbsp cold water
25 g/1 oz/2 tbsp butter

1 Using a sharp knife, make small slits in the flesh of the lamb.

2 Carefully peel the cloves of garlic and cut them into slices, using a sharp knife.

3 Push the slices of garlic into the slits in the lamb. Place the garlic-infused lamb in a shallow dish.

4 Drizzle 1 tablespoon each of the oil, sherry and soy sauce over the lamb, cover and leave to marinate for at least 1 hour, preferably overnight.

5 Using a sharp knife, thinly slice the marinated lamb.

6 Heat the remaining oil in a preheated wok. Add the lamb and stir-fry for 5 minutes.

7 Add the marinade juices and the remaining sherry and soy sauce to the wok and allow the juices to bubble for 5 minutes.

8 Mix the cornflour (cornstarch) with the cold water. Add the cornflour (cornstarch) mixture to the wok and cook, stirring occasionally, until the juices start to thicken.

9 Cut the butter into small pieces. Add the butter to the wok and stir until the butter melts. Transfer to serving dishes and serve immediately.

COOK'S TIP

Adding the butter at the end of the recipe gives a glossy, rich sauce which is ideal with the lamb.

Tuna & Vegetable Stir-Fry

Fresh tuna is a dark, meaty fish and is now widely available at fresh fish counters.
It lends itself perfectly to the rich flavours in this recipe.

Serves 4

INGREDIENTS

225 g/8 oz carrots
2 tbsp corn oil
1 onion, sliced
175 g/6 oz/2¹/₂ cups mangetout
(snow peas)

175 g/6 oz/1³/₄ cups baby corn cobs,
halved
450 g/1 lb fresh tuna
2 tbsp fish sauce
15 g/¹/₂ oz/1 tbsp palm sugar

finely grated zest and juice of
1 orange
2 tbsp sherry
1 tsp cornflour (cornstarch)
rice or noodles, to serve

1 Using a sharp knife, cut the carrots into thin sticks.

2 Heat the corn oil in a large preheated wok.

3 Add the onion, carrots, mangetout (snow peas) and baby corn cobs to the wok and stir-fry for 5 minutes.

4 Using a sharp knife, thinly slice the tuna.

5 Add the tuna to the wok and stir-fry for 2–3 minutes, or until the tuna turns opaque.

6 Mix together the fish sauce, palm sugar, orange zest and juice, sherry and cornflour (cornstarch).

7 Pour the mixture over the tuna and vegetables and cook for 2 minutes, or until the juices thicken. Serve with rice or noodles.

COOK'S TIP

Palm sugar is a thick, coarse brown sugar that has a slightly caramel taste. It is sold in round cakes or in small, round, flat containers.

VARIATION

Try using swordfish steaks instead of the tuna. Swordfish steaks are now widely available and are similar in texture to tuna.

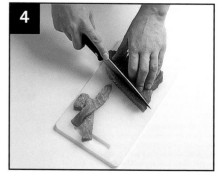

Prawns (Shrimp) with Crispy Ginger

*Crispy ginger is a wonderful garnish which offsets the spicy
prawns (shrimp) both visually and in flavour.*

Serves 4

INGREDIENTS

5 cm/2 inch piece fresh root ginger
oil, for frying
1 onion, diced
225 g/8 oz carrots, diced

100 g/3^{1}/$_2$ oz/^{1}/$_2$ cup frozen peas
100 g/3^{1}/$_2$ oz/1 cup beansprouts
450 g/1 lb peeled king prawns
(shrimp)

1 tsp Chinese five spice powder
1 tbsp tomato purée
1 tbsp soy sauce

---

1 Using a sharp knife, peel the ginger and slice it into very thin sticks.

2 Heat about 2.5 cm/1 inch of oil in a large preheated wok.

3 Add the ginger to the wok and stir-fry for 1 minute or until the ginger is crispy. Remove the ginger with a slotted spoon and leave to drain on absorbent kitchen paper. Set aside.

4 Drain all of the oil from the wok except for about 2 tablespoons.

5 Add the onions and carrots to the wok and stir-fry for 5 minutes.

6 Add the peas and beansprouts to the wok and stir-fry for 2 minutes.

7 Rinse the prawns (shrimp) under cold running water and pat dry thoroughly with absorbent kitchen paper.

8 Mix together the five spice powder, tomato purée and soy sauce. Brush the mixture over the prawns (shrimp).

9 Add the prawns (shrimp) to the wok and stir-fry for a further 2 minutes, or until the prawns (shrimp) are completely cooked through. Transfer the prawn (shrimp) mixture to a warm serving bowl and top with the reserved crispy ginger. Serve immediately.

VARIATION

*Use slices of white fish instead of
the prawns (shrimp) as an
alternative, if you wish.*

Stir-Fried Japanese Mushroom Noodles

*This quick dish is an ideal lunchtime meal, packed
with mixed mushrooms in a sweet sauce.*

Serves 4

INGREDIENTS

250 g/9 oz Japanese egg noodles
2 tbsp sunflower oil
1 red onion, sliced
1 clove garlic, crushed

450 g/1 lb mixed mushrooms
(shiitake, oyster, brown cap)
350 g/12 oz pak choi (or Chinese
leaves)

2 tbsp sweet sherry
6 tbsp soy sauce
4 spring onions (scallions), sliced
1 tbsp toasted sesame seeds

1 Place the Japanese egg noodles in a large bowl. Pour over enough boiling water to cover and leave to soak for 10 minutes.

2 Heat the sunflower oil in a large preheated wok.

3 Add the red onion and garlic to the wok and stir-fry for 2–3 minutes, or until softened.

4 Add the mushrooms to the wok and stir-fry for about 5 minutes, or until the mushrooms have softened.

5 Drain the egg noodles thoroughly.

6 Add the the pak choi (or Chinese leaves), noodles, sweet sherry and soy sauce to the wok. Toss all of the ingredients together and stir-fry for 2–3 minutes or until the liquid is just bubbling.

7 Transfer the mushroom noodles to warm serving bowls and scatter with sliced spring onions (scallions) and toasted sesame seeds. Serve immediately.

COOK'S TIP

The variety of mushrooms in supermarkets has greatly improved and a good mixture should be easily obtainable. If not, use the more common button and flat mushrooms.

Stir-Fried Green Beans with Lettuce & Blackbean Sauce

A terrific side dish, the variety of greens in this recipe make it as attractive as it is tasty.

Serves 4

INGREDIENTS

1 tsp chilli oil
25 g/1 oz/2 tbsp butter
225 g/8 oz fine green beans, sliced
4 shallots, sliced

1 clove garlic, crushed
100 g/3^1/$_2$ oz shiitake mushrooms, thinly sliced
1 Iceberg lettuce, shredded

4 tbsp blackbean sauce

1 Heat the chilli oil and butter in a large preheated wok.

2 Add the green beans, shallots, garlic and mushrooms to the wok and stir-fry for 2–3 minutes.

3 Add the shredded lettuce to the wok and stir-fry until the leaves have wilted.

4 Stir the black bean sauce into the mixture in the wok and heat through, tossing to mix, until the sauce is bubbling. Serve.

COOK'S TIP

To make your own black bean sauce, soak 60 g/2 oz/^{1}/$_3$ cup of dried black beans overnight in cold water. Drain and place in a pan of cold water, boil for 10 minutes, then drain. Return the beans to the pan with 450 ml/^{3}/$_4$ pint/2 cups vegetable stock and boil. Blend 1 tbsp each of malt vinegar, soy sauce, sugar, 1^1/$_2$ tsp cornflour (cornstarch), 1 chopped red chilli and ^{1}/$_2$ inch ginger root. Add to the pan and simmer for 40 minutes.

COOK'S TIP

If possible, use Chinese green beans which are tender and can be eaten whole. They are available from specialist Chinese stores.

Sweet & Sour Cauliflower & Coriander (Cilantro) Stir-Fry

Although sweet and sour flavourings are mainly associated with pork, they are ideal for flavouring vegetables as in this tasty recipe.

Serves 4

INGREDIENTS

450 g/1 lb cauliflower florets
2 tbsp sunflower oil
1 onion, sliced
225 g/8 oz carrots, sliced

100 g/3^{1}/$_{2}$ oz mangetout (snow peas)
1 ripe mango, sliced
100 g/3^{1}/$_{2}$ oz/1 cup beansprouts
3 tbsp chopped fresh coriander
(cilantro)

3 tbsp fresh lime juice
1 tbsp clear honey
6 tbsp coconut milk

1 Bring a large saucepan of water to the boil. Add the cauliflower to the pan and cook for 2 minutes. Drain the cauliflower thoroughly.

2 Heat the sunflower oil in a large preheated wok.

3 Add the onion and carrots to the wok and stir-fry for about 5 minutes.

4 Add the drained cauliflower and mangetout (snow peas) to the wok and stir-fry for 2–3 minutes.

5 Add the mango and beansprouts to the wok and stir-fry for about 2 minutes.

6 Mix together the coriander (cilantro), lime juice, honey and coconut milk in a bowl.

7 Add the coriander (cilantro) mixture to the wok and stir-fry for about 2 minutes or until the juices are bubbling.

8 Transfer the stir-fry to serving dishes and serve immediately.

VARIATION

Use broccoli instead of the cauliflower as an alternative, if you prefer.

Vegetable Stir-Fry

A range of delicious flavours are captured in this simple recipe which is ideal if you are in a hurry.

Serves 4

INGREDIENTS

3 tbsp olive oil
8 baby onions, halved
1 aubergine (eggplant), cubed
225 g/8 oz courgettes (zucchini), sliced

225 g/8 oz open-cap mushrooms, halved
2 cloves garlic, crushed
400 g/14 oz can chopped tomatoes
2 tbsp sundried tomato purée

freshly ground black pepper
fresh basil leaves, to garnish

1 Heat the olive oil in a large preheated wok.

2 Add the baby onions and aubergine (eggplant) to the wok and stir-fry for 5 minutes, or until the vegetables are golden and just beginning to soften.

3 Add the courgettes (zucchini), mushrooms, garlic, tomatoes and tomato purée to the wok and stir-fry for about 5 minutes. Reduce the heat and leave to simmer for 10 minutes, or until the vegetables are tender.

4 Season with freshly ground black pepper and scatter with fresh basil leaves. Serve immediately.

COOK'S TIP

Wok cooking is an excellent means of cooking for vegetarians as it is a quick and easy way of serving up delicious dishes of crisp, tasty vegetables. All ingredients should be cut into uniform sizes with as many cut surfaces exposed as possible for quick cooking.

VARIATION

If you want to serve this as a vegetarian main meal, add cubed tofu (bean curd) in step 3.

Stir-Fried (Bell) Pepper Trio with Chestnuts & Garlic

This a crisp and colourful recipe, topped with crisp,
shredded leeks for both flavour and colour.

Serves 4

INGREDIENTS

225 g/8 oz leeks
oil, for deep-frying
3 tbsp groundnut oil
1 yellow (bell) pepper, deseeded and
    diced

1 green (bell) pepper, deseeded and
    diced
1 red (bell) pepper, deseeded and
    diced

200 g/7 oz can waterchestnuts,
    drained and sliced
2 cloves garlic, crushed
3 tbsp light soy sauce

1 To make the garnish, finely slice the leeks into thin strips, using a sharp knife.

2 Heat the oil for deep-frying in a wok and cook the leeks for 2–3 minute, or until crispy. Set the crispy leeks aside until required.

3 Heat the 3 tablespoons of groundnut oil in the wok.

4 Add the (bell) peppers to the wok and stir-fry over a high heat for about 5 minutes, or until they are just beginning to brown at the edges and to soften.

5 Add the sliced waterchestnuts, garlic and light soy sauce to the wok and stir-fry all of the vegetables for a further 2–3 minutes.

6 Spoon the (bell) pepper stir-fry on to warm serving plates.

7 Garnish the stir-fry with the crispy leeks.

VARIATION

Add 1 tbsp of hoisin sauce with the soy sauce in step 5 for extra flavour and spice.

Ginger Chilli Beef with Crispy Noodles

Crispy noodles are terrific and may also be served on their own as a side dish, sprinkled with sugar and salt. Here they are complemented by the gingered chilli beef.

Serves 4

INGREDIENTS

225 g/8 oz medium egg noodles
350 g/12 oz beef fillet
2 tbsp sunflower oil
1 tsp ground ginger
1 clove garlic, crushed

1 red chilli, deseeded and very finely chopped
100 g/3½ oz carrots, cut into thin sticks
6 spring onions (scallions), sliced

2 tbsp lime marmalade
2 tbsp soy sauce
oil, for frying

1 Place the noodles in a large dish or bowl. Pour over enough boiling water to cover the noodles and leave to stand for about 10 minutes while you stir-fry the rest of the ingredients.

2 Using a sharp knife, thinly slice the beef.

3 Heat the sunflower oil in a large preheated wok.

4 Add the beef and ginger to the wok and stir-fry for about 5 minutes.

5 Add the garlic, chilli, carrots and spring onions (scallions) to the wok and stir-fry for a further 2–3 minutes.

6 Add the lime marmalade and soy sauce to the wok and allow to bubble for 2 minutes. Remove the chilli beef and ginger mixture, set aside and keep warm.

7 Heat the oil for frying in the wok.

8 Drain the noodles thoroughly and pat dry with absorbent kitchen paper. Carefully lower the noodles into the hot oil and cook for 2–3 minutes or until crispy. Drain the noodles on absorbent kitchen paper.

9 Divide the noodles between 4 serving plates and top with the chilli beef and ginger mixture. Serve immediately.

VARIATION

Use pork or chicken instead of the beef, if you prefer.

Sweet & Sour Noodles

This is a delicious Thai dish which combines sweet and sour flavours with the addition of egg, rice noodles, large prawns (shrimp) and vegetables for a real treat.

Serves 4

INGREDIENTS

3 tbsp fish sauce
2 tbsp distilled white vinegar
2 tbsp caster (superfine) or palm sugar
2 tbsp tomato purée

2 tbsp sunflower oil
3 cloves garlic, crushed
350 g/12 oz rice noodles, soaked in boiling water for 5 minutes
8 spring onions (scallions), sliced

175 g/6 oz carrot, grated
150 g/5^1/$_2$ oz/1^1/$_4$ cups beansprouts
2 eggs, beaten
225 g/8 oz peeled king prawns (shrimp)
50 g/1^3/$_4$ oz/^{1}/$_2$ cup chopped peanuts
1 tsp chilli flakes, to garnish

1 Mix together the fish sauce, vinegar, sugar and tomato purée in a small bowl. Set aside until required.

2 Heat the sunflower oil in a large preheated wok.

3 Add the garlic to the wok and stir-fry for 30 seconds.

4 Drain the noodles thoroughly and add them to the wok together with the fish sauce and tomato purée mixture. Mix well to combine.

5 Add the spring onions (scallions), carrot and beansprouts to the wok and stir-fry for 2–3 minutes.

6 Move the contents of the wok to one side, add the beaten eggs to the empty part of the wok and cook until the egg sets. Add the noodles, prawns (shrimp) and peanuts to the wok and toss together until well combined.

7 Transfer to warm serving dishes and garnish with chilli flakes. Serve hot.

COOK'S TIP

Chilli flakes may be found in the spice section of large supermarkets.

This is a Parragon Book
First published in 2003

Parragon
Queen Street House
4 Queen Street, Bath, BA1 1HE, UK

Copyright © Parragon 2003

All recipes and photography compiled from material
created by 'Haldane Mason', and 'The Foundry'.

Cover design by Shelley Doyle.

ISBN: 1-40540-838-3

Printed in China

NOTE

This book uses imperial and metric measurements. Follow the same units
of measurement throughout; do not mix imperial and metric. All spoon
measurements are level; teaspoons are assumed to be 5 ml and
tablespoons are assumed to be 15 ml. Unless otherwise stated, milk is
assumed to be whole milk, eggs and individual vegetables such as
potatoes are medium, and pepper is freshly ground black pepper.

The times given for each recipe are an approximate guide only because
the preparation times may differ according to the techniques used by
different people and the cooking times may vary as a result of the type of
oven used.

Recipes using raw or very lightly cooked eggs should be avoided by
infants, the elderly, pregnant women, convalescents and anyone suffering
from an illness.